Protecting Habitats

PROTECTING
Ocean Habitats

Anita Ganeri

GARETH**STEVENS**
GS
PUBLISHING
A Member of the WRC Media Family of Companies

Please visit our web site at: www.garethstevens.com
For a free color catalog describing Gareth Stevens Publishing's list of high-quality books
and multimedia programs, call 1-800-542-2595 (USA) or 1-800-387-3178 (Canada).
Gareth Stevens Publishing's fax: (414) 332-3567.

Library of Congress Cataloging-in-Publication Data

Ganeri, Anita, 1961-
    Protecting ocean habitats / Anita Ganeri — North American ed.
    p. cm. — (Protecting habitats)
    Includes index.
    ISBN 0-8368-4992-2 (lib. bdg.)
    1. Marine biology–Juvenile literature.   2. Ocean–Juvenile literature.   3. Habitat conservation–
Juvenile literature.   I. Title.   II. Series.
    QH91.16.G36   2005
    577.7–dc22   2005042625

This North American edition first published in 2006 by
Gareth Stevens Publishing
A Member of the WRC Media Family of Companies
330 West Olive Street, Suite 100
Milwaukee, WI 53212 USA

This U.S. edition copyright © 2006 by Gareth Stevens, Inc. Original edition copyright © 2004 by Franklin Watts.
First published in Great Britain in 2004 by Franklin Watts, 96 Leonard Street, London, EC2A 4XD. UK.

Designer: Rita Storey
Editor: Sarah Ridle
Art Director: Jonathan Hair
Editor-in-Chief: John C. Miles
Picture Research: Susan Mennell
Map and graph artwork: Ian Thompson

Gareth Stevens Editor: Gini Holland
Gareth Stevens Cover Design: Dave Kowalski

Cover image: Ecoscene
Ecoscene: pp. 9, 13, 14, 15, 19, 20, 21, 22
Science Photo Library: p.11
Still Pictures: pp. 5, 6, 7, 16, 17, 18, 23, 24, 26–27

Printed in the United States of America

1 2 3 4 5 6 7 8 9 09 08 07 06 05

CONTENTS

What Are the Oceans?

From space, our planet Earth looks blue because more than two-thirds of it is covered in seawater. This seawater lies in five oceans which, together, contain 97 percent of all the world's water. The oceans merge to form a continuous expanse of sea and provide the largest environment for living things on Earth.

The Five Oceans

In order of size, the five oceans are the Pacific, Atlantic, Indian, Southern, and Arctic. The Pacific is by far the largest, covering one-third of Earth and stretching, at its widest point, almost halfway around the world. Also the deepest, it has an average depth of about 2.5 miles (4 kilometers). It plunges to 6.8 miles (11 km) at its deepest point, in the Marianas Trench. About one-tenth the size of the Pacific, the Arctic is the smallest of the world's oceans.

It is also the shallowest, with an average depth of 0.8 miles (1.3 km). For most of the year, the Arctic Ocean is covered in a layer of floating ice, up to 10 feet (3 meters) thick.

The Origins of Oceans

About 4,600 million years ago, Planet Earth was formed from a cloud of swirling gases and dust. The great heat produced as Earth formed meant that the new planet consisted of molten (melted) rock. As it cooled and solidified, a thin, rocky crust formed. Many volcanoes covered Earth's surface at this time, releasing vast quantities of water vapor into the atmosphere. As Earth cooled further, this water vapor condensed to create storm clouds and rain. Gradually, low-lying areas filled with water to form the first oceans, which scientists think date from 3,800 million years ago.

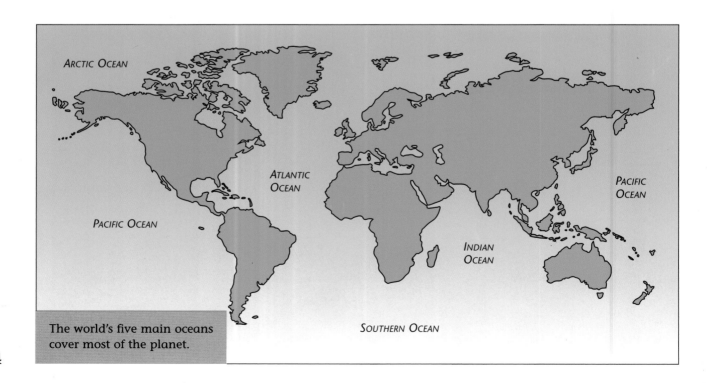

ARCTIC OCEAN

ATLANTIC OCEAN

PACIFIC OCEAN

PACIFIC OCEAN

INDIAN OCEAN

SOUTHERN OCEAN

The world's five main oceans cover most of the planet.

Today, Earth's oceans are under serious threat. Overfishing, illegal fishing, and marine pollution are just some of the major problems affecting seas all over the world. Many fish are being hunted faster than they can reproduce. These problems are destroying this fragile habitat and putting its wildlife and people in grave danger. Scientists are working hard to learn more about the sea and about how to better manage ocean resources. This book looks at some of the problems facing the oceans and at the measures being taken to study them and protect them for the future.

Salty Seawater

A key feature of seawater is its saltiness (salinity). Seawater is salty because it contains large amounts of sodium chloride, (salt). Most of this salt comes from rocks on land and is washed into the sea by rivers. Some comes from volcanoes under the sea.

Salinity is measured as the number of ounces (or grams) of salt dissolved in 2.2 pounds (one kilogram) of water. On average, 1.05 quarts (1 liter) of seawater contains about 1 ounce (35 g) of salt, although salinity varies from place to place. Salinity can be lower in places where fresh water enters the sea from melting icebergs, glaciers, and rainfall. It can be higher in warm places, where heat causes fresh water to evaporate, leaving a higher concentration of salt behind.

Under threat: A school of brightly colored fish swims past a coral formation in the Red Sea.

Under the Sea

The oceans fill enormous, bowl-shaped dips known as basins. The floor of these ocean basins, however, is not flat and featureless. There are gigantic mountain ranges, towering volcanoes, plunging valleys, and vast plains, just as there are on dry land.

Edges of Continents

Around the edges of the continents, the land slopes from the coast into the deep sea. Known as continental margins, these areas include the continental shelf, slope, and rise, which vary in width, depth, and steepness around the different continents. The continental shelf slopes gently out to sea, up to about 37 miles (60 km) from the shoreline. At the edge of the shelf, the seabed falls away steeply. This area is the continental slope, which reaches a depth of about 2 miles (3 km). Sediment flows down the slope, forming a thick layer at the bottom, called the continental rise. It slopes more gently to the seabed.

At a depth of about 2.5 to 3.5 miles (4 to 6 km), the continental margin ends and the abyssal plains begin. These vast, usually flat, plains cover over half of the ocean floor. They are carpeted in a thick layer of sediment. This sediment is formed from the bodies of billions of tiny plants and animals as well as mud, sand, and silt washed into the sea by rivers.

Seafloor Features

Earth's rocky, outer crust is split into seven huge — and many smaller — pieces called tectonic plates. These plates float like giant rafts on the semi-molten rocks beneath. As they collide or drift apart, they create dramatic seabed features and change the size and shape of the ocean basins.

Many sea animals make their homes on continental margins. Here, different forms of marine life inhabit a shipwreck.

DISCOVERING SEAMOUNTS

Seamounts are huge, extinct volcanoes which tower up from the seabed. There are as many as 30,000 seamounts scattered throughout the oceans. Until recently, little was known about life around seamounts. Now, using deep-sea video cameras, scientists are finding out more about these unique habitats. They have discovered hundreds of animal species that are new to science. Among them are sponges, sea fans, and small fish which feed from the nutrient-rich currents flowing around the seamounts.

Huge waves crash against a seamount, photographed off the coast of South America.

Where two plates pull apart under water, molten rock from deep beneath the earth rises to fill the gap. As it solidifies, it forms a new ocean crust and pushes the older crust away on either side. This is called sea-floor spreading. Over millions of years, the new crust builds mountain ranges known as spreading ridges. The longest is the Mid-Atlantic Ridge, in the Atlantic Ocean.

Although new ocean crust is constantly being made, Earth is not getting bigger. Where two plates collide underwater or at the edge of a continent, one plate is pushed downward and melts back into the earth. This is called subduction and it balances out the effect of seafloor spreading. Subduction creates long, narrow valleys, called trenches, in the seafloor.

Why Are Oceans Important?

The oceans are vitally important to our world. Millions of years ago, the earliest life on Earth began in the sea. Today, tiny ocean plants called phytoplankton produce — through the process of photosynthesis — half the oxygen we breathe. They also soak up vast quantities of carbon dioxide that would otherwise add to global warming (*see page 21*).

The oceans are home to millions of plants and animals and form the largest habitat on Earth. They also play a major part in the world's weather and climate. Ocean resources, such as oil and fish, help heat homes, run cars, and provide jobs and food.

Climate Control

The oceans are vital in regulating the world's climate. Seawater is constantly moving. The wind drives huge bands of water, called surface currents, which flow around the world. Surface currents may be as warm as 86°Fahrenheit (30° C) or as cold as 28° F (–2° C). They have a great effect on the world's climate. In the tropics, surface currents soak up the Sun's heat. They carry this heat to colder regions, then gradually release it. This action spreads heat more evenly around the world. Without surface currents, the poles would get even colder and the tropics would be unbearably hot.

Currents also affect the climate of the land masses they pass by. The Gulf Stream transports warm water from the Caribbean along the east coast of North America and then across the Atlantic Ocean to Europe. The enormous amount of heat it carries helps make the climate of northwest Europe much milder than that of places on the same latitude on the other side of the ocean.

Ocean Resources

From the oxygen we breathe to the fish we eat, the oceans are extremely rich in natural resources. Each year, about eighty-three million tons of fish are taken from the sea. Much of this is caught by modern, commercial fleets, equipped with the latest technology for locating fish shoals. About one-fifth of the oil and natural gas we use comes from under the sea. The oceans also provide transportation routes and sources of renewable energy, such as tidal power, and are popular places for leisure activities. Unfortunately, exploitation of these resources is leading to problems for the oceans and damaging these fragile habitats.

THE WATER CYCLE

The Earth's water supply is constantly recycled. The oceans play a crucial part in this process: The Sun's heat causes millions of gallons of water to evaporate from Earth's surface. This water comes from the soil, lakes, rivers, and oceans and rises into the air as water vapor. As the air rises and cools, the water vapor condenses into tiny droplets. These join to form clouds that release water as rain or snow. Some water falls in the oceans, lakes, and rivers. Some soaks into the soil. Then the water cycle begins again.

Extracting oil and gas from the seabed requires
the construction of pipelines and huge production
platforms, such as this one in the North Sea.

The Web of Life

The oceans form the largest habitat on Earth. They are home to a huge variety of living things, from tiny plants to enormous whales. Animals live in every part of the sea, from the surface water to the seabed.

Zones of Life

Different parts of the sea vary in depth, in the amount of light they receive, and in water temperature. These variations affect the type of animal living there. Scientists divide the sea into different zones of life, based on depth. The epipelagic zone reaches from the surface down to about 330 to 490 feet (100 to 150 meters). This zone's most important feature is that it is lit by the Sun, allowing plants to photosynthesize. Below this is the mesopelagic zone, also called the twilight zone. Its upper part is still light, but below about 3,200 feet (1,000 m), the water is always dark because the Sun's light cannot reach this far. The third zone, the abyssal zone, receives no sunlight at all. Here the water is always pitch black and freezing cold.

The seabed is called the benthic zone, and the animals that live here are known as the benthos. Many of them lie buried in the sediment, hidden from view. Until about one hundred years ago, scientists did not believe that anything could live below a depth of a few hundred feet. Modern technology (see page 25) has shown that benthic animals are found even at depths of over 6 miles (10 km).

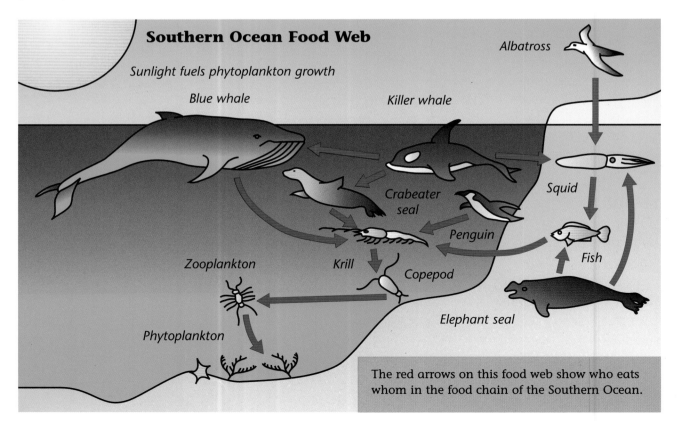

Southern Ocean Food Web

Sunlight fuels phytoplankton growth

Albatross

Blue whale

Killer whale

Squid

Crabeater seal

Penguin

Fish

Zooplankton

Krill

Copepod

Phytoplankton

Elephant seal

The red arrows on this food web show who eats whom in the food chain of the Southern Ocean.

A magnified view of marine phytoplankton shows what the entire ocean food web starts with.

Plants for Food

As on land, ocean plants and animals are linked together by what they eat. Every ocean food chain begins with microscopic, single-celled plants called phytoplankton. Because phytoplankton make their own food, grow, and multiply by photosynthesis, they are essential to life in the oceans. They are eaten by tiny zooplankton, animals which provide food for many larger animals.

Because plants need sunlight to make food, phytoplankton are only found in the upper 490 to 650 feet (150 to 200 m) of the sea. About 22,000 million tons of phytoplankton grow each year. The amount varies from place to place, being especially rich over the continental shelves. Here, the water contains plenty of nutrients, which the plants need to grow. In turn, the plants are food for large numbers of fish, so these shelves are where most of the world's catch comes from.

Plant growth is also affected by the time of year. In winter, in temperate oceans, storms whip up the water, stirring up the nutrients that rise to the surface. In spring, phytoplankton take advantage of this nutrient supply — and the longer hours of sunlight — to form enormous "blooms." These offer plenty of food for fish which, in turn, make rich pickings for seabirds and whales. By late summer, the nutrient supply runs out, so the phytoplankton die back.

The blooms color the water a cloudy green. The greener the water, the more phytoplankton it contains. Scientists are developing satellites with sensors to detect the slight changes in sea color that signify various types and quantities of phytoplankton. These satellites will allow scientists to monitor the blooms and the overall health of the oceans.

On the Edge

For plants and animals living on coasts, daily life is a struggle to survive. Every day, the shore is battered by waves, and the tides rise and fall. Coastal plants and animals must cope with being covered in water, then left high and dry. They have many special features to help them stay alive.

Battered by Waves

The shape of the world's coastlines is constantly changing as waves pound against the shore. Waves are caused by the action of the wind blowing across the surface of the sea. Stones and pebbles carried by the waves grind away at rocky coasts, wearing them away. Along some coasts, this creates dramatic features, such as arches, sea stacks, and sheer cliffs, which provide nesting sites for colonies of seabirds.

Turning Tides

Twice a day, the sea rises and floods the shore at high tide. Then it falls, or ebbs, away at low tide. The tides are mainly caused by the pull of the Moon and Sun's gravity on the oceans. This pull causes the water nearest the Moon to form a gigantic bulge, or high tide. Earth's spin pulls the oceans on the opposite side into another bulge, balancing this out.

The tidal range is the difference between the height of sea level at high and low tide. Tidal range is affected by the shape of the nearby land. Along open coasts, the tidal range is usually between 6 to 10 feet (2 to 3 m). In almost land-locked seas, such as the Mediterranean, the range is less than 3 feet (1 m). The greatest difference is in the Bay of Fundy, in southeastern Canada, which has a tidal range of over 50 feet (15 m).

Staying Alive

The intertidal zone is a tough place to live because conditions are always changing. Here, many animals filter food from the water, but, at low tide, they can no longer feed. When the tide goes out, animals are left exposed and run the risk of drying out.

Another danger for living things is being swept out to sea. Animals have evolved various methods of protection against this threat. Limpets and barnacles seal themselves in their shells and cling onto rocks. Crabs hide in damp cracks in rocks or in rock pools, while lugworms burrow in the sand.

TURTLES UNDER THREAT

All over the world, coastal regions and their wildlife are under threat from pollution and the development of tourist beaches and hotels. Sea turtles use sandy shores as nesting sites, but threats — such as habitat destruction and both humans and animals hunting for meat, eggs, and shells — wipe out thousands of turtles each year. Today, out of the seven turtle species, three face extinction, three are endangered, and the seventh is very rare.

Mussels hold onto rocks with a "beard" of strong fibers made by glands in their bodies. Fish, such as gobies, have specially adapted pelvic (rear) fins that act as suction cups. Seaweeds have strong, root-like holdfasts to anchor themselves to the rocks.

All species of sea turtle, worldwide, are now endangered. Here, a sea turtle digs a pit on a sandy beach in which to lay her eggs.

Coral Reefs

Coral reefs are the richest and most varied habitats in the sea. They are therefore sometimes compared to tropical rain forests on land. All over the world, reefs are under threat from pollution and other human activities.

Reef-Building Coral

Coral reefs are built by tiny sea animals, called coral polyps, which are related to jellyfish and sea anemones. Coral polyps' bodies contain millions of yellow-brown granules. These granules are tiny plants, called algae. The polyps and algae live in partnership. Through photosynthesis, algae provide polyps with food and oxygen. In return, the algae take in the polyps' waste products and have a safe home to live in.

Coral polyps live in huge colonies that are many millions strong. The polyps build hard, stony cases around their soft bodies, using limestone, or calcium carbonate, from the water. Each species of coral builds its protective case in a different way, resulting in an amazing variety of shapes and patterns of coral. Most of the reef is made up of cases left behind when the polyps inside die. These build up in layers, with a thin layer of living corals on top.

Life on the Reef

A coral reef is home to an astonishing range of fish and invertebrates, such as starfish, sea slugs, giant clams, and octopus. Parrot fish feed directly on the corals, nipping off pieces with their sharp, beak-like teeth.

Corals can only live in warm, shallow, tropical seas because the algae inside them need sunlight to photosynthesize.

STARFISH DANGER

The Great Barrier Reef stretches for about 1,420 miles (2,300 km) along the northeast coast of Australia. Covering some 133,000 square miles (345,000 sq km), it is the world's largest reef system. In the 1980s, large areas of coral reef were eaten away by millions of crown-of-thorns starfish. Scientists feared that the whole reef might be destroyed. Fortunately, the starfish numbers eventually decreased, leaving the reef to recover. Many environmentalists think that these swarms may happen when shell collectors upset the balance by taking too many giant triton shells, which themselves eat the starfish.

A crown-of-thorns starfish feeds on coral.

Clams and barnacles bore holes in the coral reef to hide in while they filter food from the water. Groupers are large fish which lurk in small coral caves, hardly moving. When a smaller fish comes close, the grouper strikes suddenly and seizes its prey.

Because the reef is so crowded, sea life's competition for food and space is fierce. Animals defend their territories ferociously to keep intruders away. Reef life is finely balanced between day- and night-time feeders. At daybreak, large numbers of fish leave their coral caves and holes to search for food. At sunset, they return to their hiding places and the nocturnal fish and invertebrates swarm out. Some fish, such as soldierfish, have very large eyes to help them find their prey in the dark.

Crowding is also the reason that many reef fish are so colorful. It is vital for individual fish to be able to find members of their own species so that they can pick out possible rivals and mates. The bright colors and striking patterns of reef fish, such as butter-fly fish, act as identity tags so that the fish can recognize each other.

The Open Ocean

The blue marlin, with its sword-shaped upper jaw, is one of the open ocean's greatest hunters.

The open ocean, or pelagic zone, stretches for thousands of miles beyond the continental shelves. It covers about 70 percent of Earth's surface. This huge habitat is home to some amazing animals, many of which are designed for traveling vast distances in search of food or mates.

Ocean Hunters

The open ocean is home to some of the sea's fastest and fiercest hunters, such as sharks, tuna, and marlin. They have to cover vast areas in search of prey. To hunt in their huge range as efficiently as possible, their bodies are designed as swimming machines. The blue marlin, for example, has a streamlined body shape that enables it to cut through the water, an upright dorsal (upper) fin that stabilizes its body as it swims, and crescent-shaped tail fins that propel it along at maximum speed. Its spear-like "bill" can be used for hunting, self-defense, and cutting through the water.

The sailfish — so named because of its sail-shaped first dorsal fin — is a sleek, superbly streamlined swimmer that hunts in the surface layer of tropical oceans. Over short distances, it is probably the fastest fish in the sea. It reaches speeds of over 80 miles per hour (130 km per hour) when chasing down its prey of fish and squid. Tuna are also thought to reach similar speeds.

Many species of fish group together in shoals for protection, as do these off the coast of Malaysia.

Shoals of Fish

In the open ocean, there is nowhere to hide from enemies, so prey animals have, over aeons, developed and evolved a wide range of self-defense techniques. Herring, for example, are small fish that are eaten by many ocean predators, such as dolphins and killer whales. Because they are too small to fight off their hunters individually, they swim in enormous shoals of hundreds, or even thousands, of fish. At the first sign of danger, the herring form a huge, swirling ball. This formation helps to confuse predators and makes it much harder for individual fish to be caught. The herring at the center of the ball are largely protected.

Vertical Migration

Some prey animals try to avoid predators by waiting until dark to come to the surface to feed. Scientists are still studying this process, which they call vertical migration. Every night, around dusk, millions of animals move upward from the ocean's twilight zone to the surface in search of food. At daybreak, they swim back down and spend the day out of sight of predators. The length of these migrations varies according to the animals' size. Tiny zooplankton vertically migrate only 30 to 60 feet (10 to 20 m). Larger sea animals may travel 3,000 feet (1,000 m) or more.

SHARK TAGGING

At up to 60 feet (18 m) long, whale sharks are the biggest fish in the sea. They feed on zooplankton that they sieve from the water. To locate the richest food supplies, whale sharks travel huge distances. Scientists are using satellite tags to track the whale sharks' movements. The sharks are fitted with special electronic tags that transmit information to a satellite and from there to a computer on land. Scientists can then use the data to see the sharks' range. A whale shark tagged in the Indian Ocean was found to travel almost 1,800 miles (3,000 km) in just ten days. Whale sharks are under threat from fishing, so the information collected from the tags is being used to plan a conservation program.

In the Deep

The deeper you descend in the oceans, the colder and darker the ocean water becomes. Below about 1,900 feet (600 m), there is no light at all. Here, the pressure of the water is crushing. Yet, despite these difficult conditions, an astonishing number of animals live in the ocean depths.

Finding Food

One of the main problems facing deep-sea creatures is finding food. Most deep-sea animals have adapted to take advantage of whatever food they can find. Gulper eels, for example, are found at depths of 1.2 miles (2 km) or below. Their bodies are made up mostly of huge, gaping mouths and large, stretchy stomachs, allowing them to easily swallow prey much larger than themselves. They hang in the water. Then, when their prey come close enough, they open their gigantic mouths and gulp them down.

Most of the food that reaches the deep sea consists of the dead bodies of plants and animals that fall from the surface above. Food, however, takes a very long time to sink the 3 to 6 miles (5 to 10 km) to the deep-sea floor. Scientists estimate that it takes a small dead shrimp about a week to fall just 9 feet (3 m). Much of this kind of food is eaten or rots away on the way down.

Light in the Darkness

Many deep-sea animals produce their own biological light, called bioluminescence. Some creatures make light by chemical reactions inside light-producing organs, called photophores, in their bodies. Others use bacteria living in their bodies to produce light for themselves. These lights have a number of functions. They may be used to confuse predators, to send signals to members of the same species, or to lure prey. The deep-sea angler fish has a long fin that grows in front of its mouth, like a fishing rod. At the end is a glowing blob of light, which acts like live bait, tempting prey within range of the angler fish's huge mouth.

Not a pretty sight: The deep-sea angler fish trails a lure above its mouth to attract prey.

HYDROTHERMAL VENTS

In the late 1970s, deep-sea scientists investigating the Pacific Ocean discovered springs of hot water, called hydrothermal vents, gushing up from cracks in the seabed. The vents are home to huge colonies of animals, including tube worms as big as 9 feet (3 m) long. Amazingly, these animals have their own internally contained food supply. The worms feed on bacteria living inside their bodies. In turn, the bacteria make food using minerals dissolved in the hot water. Most food chains begin with plants which use sunlight to make food. This is one of the few habitats on Earth where the inhabitants do not rely on the Sun's energy to survive.

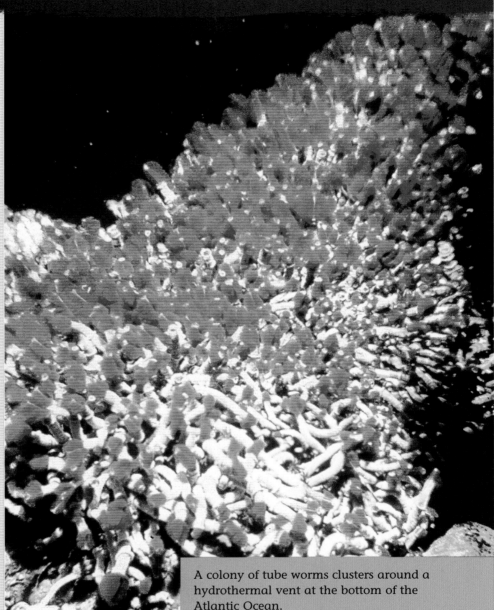

A colony of tube worms clusters around a hydrothermal vent at the bottom of the Atlantic Ocean.

Life on the Deep-Sea Floor

The amazing creatures of the deep-sea floor range from single-celled animals to worms, shrimps, starfish, and fish. Some are tiny and live buried in the sediment. Others, like sea cucumbers, crawl slowly across the sea floor, sucking up scraps to eat. Behind them, they leave criss-crossing tracks in the sediment.

The deep-sea tripod fish gets its name from its three extra-long fins. They extend underneath its body like a camera tripod. The tripod fish uses these to stand on the seabed while it waits for the current to bring it some food. Deep-sea fish are mainly black, dark-gray, or brown — these colors provide them with camouflage in the murky darkness of the deep-sea water.

19

Oceans under Threat

The world's oceans are now under tremendous pressure. Global environmental threats, such as marine pollution, drilling for oil and gas, global warming, and overfishing are damaging these fragile habitats and putting the oceans under threat.

Marine Pollution

For years, the oceans have been used as the largest garbage dump on Earth. People thought that the sheer size of the oceans could deal with whatever was dumped into them. Today, marine pollution is a serious problem. Huge amounts of industrial waste, sewage sludge, oil, and plastics are disposed of at sea every year. Most of this pollution comes from land and is washed into the sea by rivers. Much of the rest is dumped from ships or pumped directly into the sea. Sometimes oil tankers run aground and spill thousands of tons of oil. Wherever it comes from, pollution damages the oceans, killing plants and animals and harming people who rely on the sea for food.

In some places, where sewage or fertilizers wash into the sea, the water becomes covered in a thick, reddish-brown slime. This slime is known as a "red tide." It is caused by a rapid growth of red algae, which feed on nutrients in the sewage. The algae block out sunlight and starve the water of oxygen so that fish and other animals suffocate.

Rescue workers struggled to save oil-soaked wildlife after a tanker, the *Prestige*, ran aground off the coast of Spain in 2002 and spilled its cargo.

EXTRACTING OIL AND GAS

About one-fifth of the world's oil and gas comes from under the sea. Since 1947, when the first offshore oil rig was set up in the Gulf of Mexico, oil and gas exploration has become extremely big business. By the mid-1990s, there were almost 6,500 oil and gas platforms. Most of the platforms are found on the continental shelves. Now, with the growing demand for oil and gas, it seems likely that companies will want to drill in deeper and deeper waters. Environmentalists are concerned about the effects of this drilling on the fragile and unique deep-ocean habitat.

Global Warming

Many scientists believe that Earth is getting warmer because of what they call the greenhouse effect. Small amounts of carbon dioxide (CO_2) and other "greenhouse" gases are found naturally in the atmosphere. Like the glass in a green-house, these gases help trap the Sun's heat, keeping Earth warm enough for life. Burning fossil fuels, such as oil and gas, is increasing the amount of CO_2. The extra CO_2 is trapping too much heat and making Earth too warm. Increased warming may also be partly due to natural climate change. If this warming trend continues, by the year 2100, Earth's temperature may have risen by about 4° Fahrenheit (2° C). This temperature would melt the ice at the poles, raising sea levels by some 160 feet (50 m) and drowning low-lying coastal areas and islands around the world.

Many scientists are also worried that the extra CO_2 is reacting with sea-water and making the oceans too acidic. This process is happening too quickly for the oceans to adjust naturally. Experts are not yet sure how this might affect ocean wildlife. Many think that coral may be at greatest risk. The acid could dissolve the calcium carbonate that corals use to make their protective cases.

Seabirds and other creatures living on coasts are very vulnerable to oil spills.

Coral Reefs at Risk

All over the world, coral reefs are at risk. One-quarter of the world's reefs has already been destroyed. Another 60 percent are seriously threatened by human activities, such as pollution, mining for sand and rock, and harvesting rare corals and shells. Fishing boats also smash and destroy reefs.

Another major threat to coral reefs is coral bleaching. Much of the corals' color comes from the algae living inside the coral polyps. When the sea gets warmer, the algae die or the corals themselves push them out. Before long, the whole reef turns ghostly white. Coral bleaching may be the result of disease, lack of sunlight, or a change in salinity. The most likely cause, however, is global warming (*see p 21*). If the water cools, the corals may recover. If, on the other hand, all the algae is lost, the corals will die and the reefs crumble. Scientists estimate that, by the end of the twenty-first century, coral bleaching will have killed half of the world's remaining reefs.

Coral reef destruction has a devastating effect on wildlife. Not only wildlife is at great risk, however. In many poorer parts of the world, millions of people along the coasts rely on coral reefs for their food, building materials, and livelihoods. In Asia alone, coral reefs are home to about one-quarter of all the fish caught. Millions of tourists visit reefs each year to dive or snorkel, and this provides local people with much-needed income. The reefs also play a valuable part in protecting the shoreline from storm surges and erosion. Losing the reefs could spell disaster for these coastal communities.

Coral reefs — surrounding islands such as this one — are threatened in many different ways.

Overfishing

For centuries, people have relied on the sea for food. Millions of tons of fish and shellfish are caught every year. Many modern commercial fishing boats are equipped with computers, satellites, and radar for locating fish, allowing them to catch more fish than ever. Today, overfishing is a serious problem that is now upsetting the natural balance of the ocean habitat. So many fish are being caught that there is not enough time for the fish to breed and grow and for stocks to recover again. Many of the world's fisheries are overfished or on the edge of collapse. Fish that we once took for granted, such as cod, tuna, and salmon, are no longer common. Between the years 2001 and 2002, the total weight of cod in the North Sea, for example, plummeted from 56,000 tons to 42,000 tons. If this trend continues, cod will die out for good.

DOLPHIN-FRIENDLY TUNA

Thousands of sea animals, like the dolphin shown below, are killed when they accidentally get caught up in fishing gear. They are known as by-catch. Tuna are one of the world's most valuable and popular types of fish for human consumption. They often swim with large schools of dolphins, following them to find food. By chasing the dolphins, which come up for air, fishing boats could find the tuna and set a net around tuna and dolphins alike. Following public protest in the 1980s, this form of fishing was banned and the number of dolphin deaths reduced. Unfortunately, many other animals, such as sharks, remain by-catch.

What Is Being Done?

Exploring the deep: A ship-board scientist operates the controls of an ROV (remotely operated vehicle) on a research mission.

Around the world, many conservation groups, scientists, and governments are working hard to understand the oceans better in order to protect them and their unique wildlife. The oceans form such a vast habitat that, despite modern technology, we still know little about them. Faced with the growing threats to the oceans, it is vital to find out more.

Exploring the Oceans

Until about fifty years ago, scientists had little idea about what lay beneath the sea. Today, there is still a vast amount of ocean to be explored, and scientists have developed cutting-edge technology which allows them to investigate deeper than ever before.

Sound travels quickly through water. This is why ocean scientists often use sonar to map the deep-sea floor. Sonar instruments work by giving out sharp "bleeps" of sound. These hit parts of the seabed and send back echoes. From the pattern of these echoes, scientists can build up a picture of the sea floor, including features such as seamounts and trenches.

Scientists also use sound to keep in contact with instruments deep in the ocean. These instruments respond to sound signals sent to them by ships many miles away. Some are left in place on the seabed for over a year to collect samples or take measurements. They are attached to long wires, weighted down on the seabed and fixed to air-filled floats. When they receive a sound signal, the wires are released from the weights. The floats bring the instruments to the surface, where they are picked up by the research ship.

Deep-Sea Submersibles

A submersible is an underwater vehicle, like a miniature submarine, used to explore the deep sea. Some submersibles are unmanned robots or ROVs (remotely operated vehicles), which carry cameras and other sampling and measuring equipment. Some are attached to a research ship by a cable along which information and instructions are sent. Free-swimming submersibles are also being developed. They will carry their own power supply and send data back to land through satellite links.

Ocean research is also helped by manned submersibles that can carry scientists deep beneath the sea. The *Johnson Sealink II* is a modern, manned submersible, launched in Florida. It is designed to carry a crew of four and operate at depths down to 1.8 miles (3 km). The submersible is fully equipped with a range of instruments, which include suction devices, plankton samplers, and sonar as well as both still and video cameras. To see in dark water, it uses powerful arc lights, which can create almost-daylight conditions.

Satellite Surveys

Satellites high above Earth also observe the oceans. They have revolutionized ocean science because they can gather information much more quickly than research ships. Among other things, the data collected has allowed scientists to make detailed maps showing sea surface temperature and the patterns of ocean currents, and it also helps them monitor changes in sea levels and the size and location of phytoplankton blooms.

A new satellite, *Aqua*, was launched by the United States in 2002. It is being used to study cloud features and phytoplankton and to collect information about the water cycle. From this, scientists are hoping to learn more about the connection between the oceans and climate change.

Saving the Seas

Conservation groups, such as Greenpeace, the Worldwide Fund for Nature (WWF), and Conservation International are working hard to save the oceans from further harm. Since the 1980s, Greenpeace has been campaigning to stop the dumping of oil — including that from gas rigs — and radioactive waste in the sea. The WWF's "Endangered Seas"

campaign is aimed at protecting marine habitats by reducing pollution, stopping the illegal trade in ocean wildlife, and ending destructive fishing methods. The WWF works with governments around the world to help find ways for people to use the oceans without causing lasting harm. It also wants to see the introduction of more Fishing-Free Zones. These are areas closed to fishing where fish stocks can recover.

In April 2004, the WWF and Greenpeace won an important victory in their campaign to protect the Baltic Sea. The International Maritime Organization (IMO) decided to mark the sea as a "Particularly Sensitive Sea Area." The Baltic is one of the world's busiest,

well-traveled seas, and oil spills from ship accidents are threatening the sea and its wildlife, particularly fish and migrating birds. The new measures mean that ships must take extra care, reducing the risk of accidents.

Protected Areas

One way of saving the oceans may be to set aside certain areas as protected marine parks. These would safeguard endangered species and fish stocks, while at the same time making sure that local people can still earn a living. The challenge is to find a balance between ocean protection and commercial exploitation. At present, only about 0.5 percent of the oceans is protected. One of the places earmarked for protection is the area around the hydrothermal vents off the Azores islands in the Atlantic Ocean. Conservation organizations are also working with the tourist industry to make sure that divers and other visitors do not damage sensitive habitats.

Some marine parks are already well established. The Great Barrier Reef Marine Park in Australia, set up in 1975, covers about 133,530 square miles (345,950 sq km). The reef is also on the United Nation's list of World Heritage Sites. It is home to at least 4,000 species of mollusk, 1,500 species of fish, and 400 species of coral, many of them severely endangered. Even with protection, the fragile reef system remains under threat from fishing, pollution, and global warming.

National parks can help preserve huge areas of coral reef from destructive activities. This is part of the Great Barrier Reef Marine Park in Australia.

Further Information

International Agreements

There are many agreements, treaties, and organizations in place to protect the oceans and safeguard their special resources and wildlife. These are just a few of them.

1. UNCLOS (United Nations Convention on the Law of the Sea) (1982)

Internationally recognized, this treaty deals with all matters concerning the law of the sea and lays down a full set of rules to protect and preserve the marine environment. It includes rules for the safe and sustainable use of the oceans and their resources and for preventing and reducing marine pollution. It also promotes the efficient and peaceful use of the oceans.

2. OSPAR (Convention for the Protection of the Marine Environment of the Northeast Atlantic) (1992)

Signed by fourteen European countries bordering the northeast Atlantic, this treaty — covering the coastal oil-producing states of Western Europe — calls on members "to take all possible steps to prevent and eliminate pollution" and to "take the necessary measures to protect the maritime area against the adverse effects of human activities."

3. MARPOL (International Convention for the Prevention of Pollution from Ships) (1973)

This convention provides a full set of international guidelines to deal with ocean dumping and to prevent pollution from ships. It contains six sections and covers oil pollution, the disposal of sewage from ships, plastics and garbage, and air pollution.

4. UNFA (United Nations Fisheries Agreement) (2001)

An international treaty for conserving world fisheries and protecting ocean wildlife, this agreement aims to protect fish species, such as tuna, cod, pollock, hake, and halibut, which are in danger of being overfished. It also seeks to reduce by-catch and waste in fishing and to collect information on fish catches.

5. The New Common Fisheries Policy (2002)

This policy sets out a framework for fishing in Europe to stop overfishing and protect the marine environment. Among the main points of the agreement are:
1. Fewer new fishing boats to be built after 2004.
2. A more environmentally friendly approach to fisheries' management with recovery plans for endangered fish stocks.
3. Greater help with the scrapping of fishing boats to reduce the size of fishing fleets.

6. CITES (Convention on International Trade in Endangered Species) (1975)

CITES works to ban international trade in an agreed list of endangered species, including marine animals such as sea turtles. It monitors and regulates trade in other species that run the risk of becoming endangered.

7. UNFCCC (United Nations Framework Convention on Climate Change) (1992)

Signed by over 160 countries at the Rio Earth Summit, this convention recognizes that climate change affects the whole of the planet, including the oceans, and aims to reduce the levels of greenhouse gases being produced by human activities.

8. ICRAN (International Coral Reef Action Network) (2000)

This partnership of several international organizations works to stop and reverse the damage being done to the world's coral reefs, looks at ways of monitoring and managing reefs, and considers ways to agree on a framework for conservation. It also aims to raise people's awareness about the threats facing the reefs.

Web Sites

Here are a few Web sites to help you to find out more about the oceans:

www.whoi.edu
Explore the Web site of the Woods Hole Oceanographic Institution in the United States, with its information on all aspects of marine science.

www.hboi.edu
Click on Marine Operations on the home page of the Harbor Branch Oceanographic Institution and then on the link to the Johnson Sealink II submersible to take a virtual deep sea trip .

www.soc.soton.ac.uk
Discover the Southampton Oceanography Centre in the UK and gain information about marine science and marine technology.

www.marine.csiro.au
Read current information about Australia's marine resources and the efforts being made to conserve them.

seawifs.gsfc.nasa.gov/ocean_planet. html
Take virtual tour of the oceans at the Smithsonian Institution.

www.panda.org
Learn about the World Wildlife Fund (WWF) — or Worldwide Fund for Nature International — and details of their latest campaigns and conservation hot spots.

www.greenpeace.org
Explore Greenpeace's current ocean projects and get updates on previous campaigns.

www.earthwatch.unep.net/oceans
Gain information on this Web site about the world's most endangered places, including the oceans and the coral reefs.

Glossary

abyssal
the part of the deep ocean that lies below 1.2 miles (2 km)

adapted
having certain features or ways of behaving which allow a plant or animal to survive in a particular habitat

aeons
large divisions of geological time, usually longer than eras

algae
a group of simple plants, ranging from tiny, one-celled plants to huge seaweeds

bacteria
microscopic, single-celled living things found in all environments

benthic
describes the seabed

benthos
the animals living on the seabed

bioluminescence
light made by plants and animals

carbon dioxide
a gas, found in the atmosphere, that is released when animals breathe out or when fuel, such as coal or wood, burns; it is absorbed by plants when they photosynthesize

condensed
the state of water when water vapor cools and turns into liquid water

endangered
animals and plants that are in danger of dying out or becoming extinct

epipelagic
describing the top layer of the sea, which is the top 330 to 490 feet (100 to 150 m)

erosion
the wearing out and shaping of the land by weather and the action of the sea

evaporated
when liquid water is heated and turns into water vapor

extinction
when an animal or plant dies out forever

fisheries
known areas for catching particular breeds of fish

intertidal
the part of a coast that lies between the high-tide mark and the low-tide mark

invertebrates
animals that do not have backbones or skeletons inside their bodies

latitude
the measure of distance, in 90-degree intervals, of how far a place is to the north or the south of the equator

mesopelagic
describing the part of the sea that lies at a depth of between 600 to 3,000 feet (200 and 1,000 m)

nutrient
a substance in food that plants and animals need to stay alive

pelagic
describing the open ocean, the water that lies above the seabed

photosynthesis
the process by which green plants take in sunlight, CO_2, and water to make oxygen and food

phytoplankton
microscopic, single-celled plants that drift in the sea and form the basis, or bottom, of most ocean food chains

renewable energy
sources of energy that can be used again and again

salinity
the saltiness of seawater

sea stacks
pillars of land that remain when wave action against a coast creates caves that erode into natural tunnels; when the arches over the tunnels collapse, the pillars, or sea stacks, remain

sediment
particles of sand, gravel, clay, mud, and silt that are washed into the sea from rivers and that settle on the seabed

sonar (Sound Navigation And Ranging)
a method or device that detects the position or geography of an area by sending out sounds and mapping the pattern of the returning echoes

storm surges
very high sea levels caused by strong winds blowing across the surface of the water

temperate oceans
oceans that lie between the constantly warm tropical waters around the equator and the waters at the cold poles

vertical migrations
daily journeys made by animals that travel up through the layers of the sea

water vapor
water in the form of a gas

zooplankton
tiny sea animals that graze on phytoplankton and in turn become food for fish and other sea animals that are higher on the ocean food chain

Index